Thelema Magick Explained

Thelema Magick Guide for Beginners

Thelema Magick Overview, Aliester Crowley, Basics Rituals, Daily Magickal Regimen, Elemental Tools, Phases of Magickal Rituals, How to Discover One's True Will and More!

By Riley Star

Foreword

This book is about giving you the brief overview of
Thelema Magick and its principle based from Aleister
Crowley. He is one of the most important figures of magick
and occultism. According to him, magick can be defined as
the "art and science of causing change to occur in conformity
with the will become axiomatic." Crowley's teaching is
focused on finding one's true will, which he believed is
something that stems out from one's core being; thus
defining one's true nature – your true calling, purpose or
whatever you want to call it – is instrumental in knowing
your true self.

Aside from his teachings, Aleister Crowley also
helped popularized the use of psychedelics, drugs, and also
sex magick during rituals. He also combined the western
and eastern elements as well as philosophized the how's and
why's of Thelema magick along with the different
symbolisms used during the magick rituals. Crowley had
become a huge influenced especially to the students of

Thelema magick and traditions, as well as other fields of studies and relating to occultism. Aleister Crowley is one of the most notorious figures of modern magick, and through this book, you'll get to learn some of the basic teachings and principles he taught. Whatever your view of Crowley as a person, it's important to note that if you are really interested in this subject, your mind and heart should be open to his occult teachings, the developments he made in the subject Thelema magick, and his principles so that you can fully understand what you're trying to learn; after all, his teachings are the ones who stood the test of time.

There's a lot of false information online about Thelema magick or the teachings of Crowley which is why the purpose of this book is to provide you with unbiased information, and also to look at all the basic aspects of his philosophies and teachings. However, we can only provide you with a brief overview or just an introduction about the world of Thelema magick because as much as we'd like to discuss everything in depth, it's quite impossible because the subject tackles on different aspects. If you're really serious about learning Crowley's philosophy or other teachings related to Thelema magick, you can read tons of books personally written by him, and other great resources that you can avail online or can be found in your local libraries.

This book will provide you with the basic overview of what Thelema magick is all about, its significance, core principles, basic practices, rituals and the likes.

Table of Contents

Introduction to Thelema Magick

The very core of Aleister Crowley's occult principles and teachings is the Will (Thelema). Thelema is the greek word of one's will. Crowley's philosophy can be summed up into a phrase which is "thou without wilt, shall be the whole of the law." If you will join occult groups that study this field, or people who follow the teachings of Crowley, you'll soon find out that this phrase is also what the students/practitioners (often called Thelemites) say to greet each other. The phrase however, is often misunderstood and misinterpreted especially by those who aren't really a serious student of this subject. This introductory chapter will give you a glimpse of what is the real meaning of the phrase aforementioned, and how it is related to the core principle found in Crowley's teachings with regards to Thelema Magick.

What is the Will?

As what we've mentioned earlier, the phrase "thou without wilt, shall be the whole of the law" is often misinterpreted as something equivalent to doing whatever one wants. However, if you read in depth the works of Crowley, you'll realize that it's not what he meant at all. The phrase refers to one's true will, and one's true will refers to a person's purpose in life. It means to discover who you are at the deepest core of your being.

If you become a follower of Crowley's teachings or what's known as Thelemites, your mission is to discover and also accomplish your "true will." In layman's terms, true will is about matching your natural talents and core being with what the universe need. This is your purpose, your life's calling, your true nature that's aligned with your identity, personal values, and natural gift; it's perhaps something that's concern with your place in the universe, and it's all about finding your true path. If you want to know in depth what the meaning of true will is based on Crowley's teaching then make sure that you read the two important texts he wrote; these are "The Law of Liberty" and "The Message of the Master Therion," these texts are available online, or can be found in your local library. We highly recommend you read it because it's also central to understanding what Crowley means when it comes to true will.

The will is the dynamic or active aspect of oneself. You have to have knowledge of your true self; it's akin to the old saying "thou shall know thyself." Knowing your will is also related to self – actualization which is the highest need in Maslow's Hierarchy of Needs.

How Does One Discover The Will?

There had been many texts written discussing the theoretical side of the Thelema philosophy as well as its practical side but when it comes to the actual question of how a person can truly discover his/her will, most of these writings fall short. Within the Thelemic community, such discussions and questions only lead to the inquirer being told to just keep learning and practicing it the various forms of ceremonial magick or do rituals etc. However, given the fact that the will is the core principle of the Thelema, it's quite interesting that some Thelemites pay no attention as to why such rituals or exercises should be done, how such practices can lead in finding one's will, or what the discovery of one's will entails to life in general.

There are lots of self – professed Thelemites as well as experienced ones that aren't able to fully explain what the will is when they are being asked. Sometimes, such Thelemites only has a faith – based approach. This could be fatal for those who wish to practice such art or those who are sincerely aspiring to be one because usually, students are encouraged to just put their faiths in dubious rituals or practices without knowing in layman's terms precisely what it is that one is supposed to be finding or achieving in the process.

This is what we want to accomplish in this book. We want to show you the theoretical/ philosophical side based from Crowley's teachings, and also state in plain layman's term about the nature of finding one's will, and perhaps provide some practical guidance on how to approach such undertaking so that you can have a glimpse of what this subject is all about, and learn to use it in your daily lives.

Chapter One: The Essence of Finding One's Will

The practical side of Thelema according to Crowley's philosophy can be summed into these two phrases: (1) "Thou must find out what is thy Will, "and (2) Do the Will with detachment, focus, and peace. In this case, simplifying such principles can become more obscuring than clarifying because such phrases assumes that a person already know what is meant by 'Will'. However, as what we've pointed out in the introduction, the Will is the central or core idea behind the whole Thelema philosophy yet it's also the most widely misunderstood. Thelemites should first totally understand what the Will means so that they can truly grasp the idea behind the philosophy that they're practicing. This is what we're going to teach you in this chapter.

The Most Essential Concept of Thelema

Will is the dynamic or active expression of a person's preferences in life. As an example, if you come to think about it, many people like to eat food that's delicious, we all like to drink water or good beverages, and also have a comfortable place to stay that can protect us from various outside elements which is why in most cases, a person's will also involves one's tendency to meet such basic needs. Beyond this, one may be inclined towards various physical and intellectual stimulations or activities, or towards one's passion and creative pursuits. One may also like or dislike going to different places, learning different subjects, and developing various skill set. The point here is that, there are infinite possibilities for what can comprise the Will of a person. It's as endless as the uniqueness of each individual, and regardless of the details, the set of circumstances that comprises the Will depends on the different tendencies of certain types of activities an individual is engaged in or would want to engage in, and it's also based on one's unique nature.

If you put the Will in these terms then the whole concept about it becomes simple right? After all, everybody is naturally inclined to do anything every day of their live. If that's the case, what is then so special about this idea?

Many self – professed Thelemites interpret knowing one's Will as a representation of some kind of 'higher purpose,' perhaps a strict path or a practical imperative to follow that's ordained by the cosmos, and functions as sort of a moral obligation. Such interpretation is quite displeasing because a cursory examination will reveal that there's an absence of any cosmic ordination which compels us to strive for unnatural aims. So let's simplify it without taking out the actual interpretation of the concept of Will.

"Do what thou wilt" doesn't mean that one should do what one likes. It doesn't also imply that the preferences we have, like what we've mentioned in the examples, is also wrong rather it implies that we think we want something else. You see, the problem is not the preferences of a person, the problem is that most times, people aren't aware of what those preferences are, and it's usually because it's masked by false 'wants and needs' that's manufactured in our minds.

You may have heard this before but you should understand that most times, *what we think we want is different from what we actually want.* And this is because most often than not, people aren't aware of their 'true' preferences, and if you're not fully aware, the mind will create a web of illusory wants and needs, thereby confusing oneself when it comes to choosing preferences.

If however, your mind could replace such false wants or needs with true preferences then the phrase "Do what thou wilt" would indeed mean 'doing what you want or like.'

Practical Situations

Many people believe that they know what they actually want but based on experiences, studies, and real life examples, the vast majority are usually and consistently wrong. Throughout history, people will seem to achieve what they thought they wanted but in the end it fails to satisfy them because it turns out that's not what they wanted at all. The job, the dream, the money, the kind of life that they thought would make them happy or satisfied is most often than not just false illusory of their minds, and it's because they don't know their true preferences thus not knowing their true Will.

The saying, "the grass is always greener on the other side" is one example that the desire of a person is not actually driven by their true preferences but by the mere absence of such true preferences.

As an example, you'll see that billions of dollars are spent in advertising by many companies and businesses that aim to convince people of the things they really don't want.

Then there's also this modern phenomenon popularly known as the 'mid – life crisis' which usually arises because one realizes that the things they work hard for all their lives or the things they have achieved is not really what they like to have, and it's mostly because such achievement is motivated by something else other than their own preferences whether it's a perceived need like financial security, or through false values instilled at a young age by other people like your parents or friends, or by the seemingly attractive alternatives offered by outside parties.

The fact remains that the average person today has no idea what his/her true preferences are and it's perhaps because they don't practice self – awareness especially when it comes to making decisions about what they want or don't want. This is the reason why most people just blindly follow false desires.

Significance of Discovering "True Will"

For you to be aligned with your true preferences or your true Will, you should first ask yourself why you do what you do, why you choose this or that, and what's the reason behind your decisions? Is it because somebody told you to do such things, or perhaps you're influenced by outside factors, or is this something that's just passed on to you by other people without you making due diligence?

This is the start of self – awareness which can help you find your true preferences, and eventually your true Will.

The problem with an average student of any occult is that they are not aware of their own preferences because there's a strong influence among other occultists. Their own preferences are being clouded with one web of confusion after another by their fellow 'experienced' occultists and teachers. Such people convince their students and themselves that they have achieved some sort of clarity. If you are a new student or have recently became a member of an occult, it's probably best to make sure that the leaders you're following are people who will explain to you in simple terms the reason why you're doing what you're doing, and the significance of this practice. Otherwise, you should be careful as to what you're listening to.

The question of 'finding one's will' is therefore not about identifying what the cosmos prepared for you or the ordained path that you should take. Finding or discovering your Will is perhaps the act of clearing away the false desires, wants or needs created by your mind or influenced by other people which diverts you from acting in alignment with your true self – preference. You have to be free from such illusory influences because that is what will ultimately lead you in knowing your True Will.

The Will and the phrase "Do what thou Wilt," doesn't denotes some sort of special consecrated course that the Universe or 'God' place in your life. There may be a path that your inclined to do or that is set forth for you but if you want to discover it and follow your true preferences, your job is to distinguish and liberate yourself from 'false Will' that's contained in your mind or from other external factors, otherwise the complexity and ubiquity of such false Will can make it difficult for you to discover your own path. This task of clearing your mind in order to find your truest will is the real core of Thelemic practice.

Chapter Two: The Nature of the Will

As what we've emphasized in the previous chapter, clearing out such illusory needs and wants off of one's mind is the main aspect of Thelemic practice. However, this is not the complete description. A lot of people say that 'our minds is often our greatest enemy,' and if you think about it, the mind indeed is the one responsible for veiling one's will. Whenever we do something, it is natural for us to use our minds, which is why it's impossible to completely shut it down. What one must do in order to find and follow one's will is to use the mind to the service of it. It's not enough to just clear off the mind with unnecessary clutter of preferences; one should also learn to make it become aware of the true preferences, and be able to train it so that it will not become a distraction with the perception of one's will.

Using the Mind in Alignment to the Will

The main role of the mind is to train it to become aware of your own preferences because this is what will lead to discovering your True Will. It's not about knowing what to do; it's more about knowing why you do what you do. The will can be made apparent if you pay attention to it instead of paying attention to the mind. The main purpose of why you need to make your mind aware of your True Will is not just so that your mind can create a representation of your will that could guide you, but rather make your mind assist or help you in the fulfillment of your own will.

For example, if your Will says that you want to move from one city to another, it'll be impossible to achieve that task without your mind's assistance right? At the same time, the mind can't also accomplish such task unless it knows that moving to another city is your true desire.

If you put it in another perspective, your objective could never be your True Will unless you are aware of what it's like living in another city or if such city exists, and such knowledge came from your mind. From this example, you can see that both the mind and the Will work together. Both of them should be aligned with one another. However, even if the mind contributes knowledge to the process, the mind cannot distinguish the true preference of the self, only the Will does that.

It is possible to find out what your Will is but it's impossible to square it out, so to speak. Your Will can never be found through thinking or working out. It's never found through analysis because one must 'know thy will' before you even use your mind to think about it. You don't figure out what your Will is because then it becomes a mental process; the mind can't become aware of True Will by attending to its own processes, it should be informed by something that's external. To reiterate, your mind should be capable of consciously representing your True Will but not in a way of knowing what to do, instead the mind should just help you know how to do it, how to fulfill your Will.

Perhaps in layman's terms, the Will can be something that's coming naturally from one's heart or from one's innermost being. It's not something you find because it's already within, and you need to use your mind to figure out how you can fulfill such Will.

Training the Mind

In order to fulfill your True Will, a person must learn how to train his/her mind. This is what comprises the bulk of Thelemic practice.

The first thing you need in order to accomplish this is to give your mind a comprehensive general education. If you want to have the maximum chance of fulfilling your True Will then you need to ensure that your mind has a good knowledge of the opportunities and methods for doing so.

A simple example to illustrate this point is that, the self can't satisfy its basic need for food, if the mind doesn't have knowledge of what a food is in the first place, and materials like plants and animals can be cooked or eaten. Even if your mind has knowledge about such things, your Will may still remain unfulfilled because you have no idea which animals and plants to eat, or the methods on how one can eat them. Of course such 'knowledge' may come from basic instinct as a human being, but it still resides entirely on the mind, if it has enough knowledge about agriculture, food manufacturing etc., which can increase the likelihood of success or the fulfillment of one's Will.

A mind that's also hampered with false knowledge, beliefs, notions of morality, and the likes will be far less able to help in the fulfillment of one's self preferences, and if that'll be the case as in some people, it will be difficult for them to come to terms with their self - preferences or True Will in matters like relationships or sexuality leaving them unsatisfied and perhaps unhappy.

The second most important thing after letting your mind learn as much as you can about life in general is to train it to become aware. Usually, this is the most essential thing why people fail to know what they truly desire, it's because they don't have self – awareness. You need to be able to question your own mind or your own self whenever you're making decisions or choices in anything. The Will becomes apparent if one learns how to observe the interactions of one's self and its environment especially if it's free from the influences of the mind.

According to Crowley, one should obtain the emancipation of thought by putting each idea against its opposite, and refuse to prefer either. Can you imagine the difficulties that a person will experience if for example, one insisted of connecting all 3 wires to the same pin of a 3 – pronged plug because he/she just 'prefers' it this way. However sometimes, our own preferences interferes our ability to truly perceive something with clarity due to lack of self - awareness.

This is why it's quite essential to put your ideas against its opposite and not make any preference so that your mind can learn to avoid being influenced by your own perception of accepting one idea over the other. You should see things as they are rather than how you prefer them to be. Your mind should be trained to also distinguish what is real and what is imaginary through altering your own personal process of judgment, or simply becoming aware of it.

Practical Application

Here's a good example to illustrate the importance of training your mind, and practicing self – awareness so that you can fulfill your True Will:

Suppose you're out on the lake, it's a bit foggy, and you're rowing in your own little boat having a nice time by yourself. Suddenly, out of nowhere, you see another rowboat coming out of the fog, and boom! Your boat crashes with this another rowboat. You instantly became angry because you just recently painted your boat, and you're thinking what kind of fool crashes a rowboat, but then the fog clears, and you realize there's no one riding that rowboat. After realizing this, your anger towards this 'other person' (that doesn't exist at all) suddenly fades away and you accept that it's a complete accident.

Such example clearly shows how our minds interpret the same event in different ways, thanks to our minds' imagination. This is exactly how your mind imposes its own interpretation in your perception. The anger you felt is not because of the event, it's a reaction of your mind – of whatever it imagined. You might have felt afraid and not angry, but the rowboat is still empty, and there's really nothing to be afraid of yet your mind influenced your perception to make you feel such a thing through its imagination of why the boat could've crashed into yours.

Faulty Interpretations and Perceptions

The aforementioned situation is a great example of how our minds make things seem 'real' when in fact; it's just our mere imaginations. This is also one of the problems that aspiring Thelemites face; one usually mistakes imaginary preferences for the real preferences of oneself. And until a person is aware of such thing, he/she wouldn't be able to correct it. This is why self – awareness is important, this is why you should question yourself from time to time, and find out why you do what you do, why you feel what you feel, and why you're thinking what you're thinking. Questioning the mind and its influences to your perception can help you in identifying what is real and what's imaginary or what's just placed unto you by other external factors.

In short, you must train your mind to be aware of how in itself distorts and influences your perception and 'reality.' It's not enough to just obtain general knowledge of how your mind does it, you must learn to identify in what way your mind influences your perceptions, and catch doing it in real time. Once your mind gets caught up on its own, it must then work on lessening such tendencies or influences in order to avoid it obscuring reality.

When you or your mind becomes aware of itself whenever it's distorting your perception, it will become proficient at it, and with time enable itself to identify such distortions when it happens. This will make your mind remove or avoid having faith in its own faulty imaginations or interpretations.

Once the mind becomes quite proficient at it, it should then observe the interactions between oneself, and the environment to gain clarity, and not because it is what you/ your mind prefers. Over time, you'll see patterns of how the self informs the mind of its true preferences.

The mind can eventually be reliable enough to be put into the service of fulfilling one's True Will. It will unlock your innermost desires, and it'll be aligned with the core of your being. Such fundamental concepts are the real essence of what Thelemic practice is all about. This is also what Crowley is trying to explain to any aspiring Thelemite. Unfortunately, some occultist most often than not, teach faulty interpretations to new students (because they themselves aren't fully aware, and their interpretations is mostly based on their own preferences), and makes them believe that for one to find or discover one's True Will, ceremonial magick rituals are necessary. This of course, stems out because some occultists are completely ignorant of what the Will really is, and how to unlock it.

Modifying Your Own Mind

Based on what we've discussed all throughout this chapter, the conclusion for this is that there's no 'standard system' of how one can modify their faulty minds or perhaps how one can have self – awareness. You have to understand that even if there are commonalities or patterns, the details of how a mind distorts or gives faulty perceptions will vary from one individual to another. Training one's mind to perceive such details will also vary, and the approach must be tailored to each individual. Therefore, the individual himself is the only one who has the 'power' to effectively identify and tailor the approach when it comes to improving one's mind. That being said, there are various and simple ways on how one can effectively handle such distortions of reality caused by the untrained mind which will highly benefit an aspiring Thelemite and also the 'experienced' ones. Such practices that we will discuss in the next few chapters will help improve one's mind in developing self – awareness, and it will also help each individual to modify such practices and help him/her to design his/her own.

Chapter Three: Quiet Awareness

The first simple exercise you can do can be done through quiet awareness. The purpose of this practice is to simply develop one's mind when it comes to becoming aware of the environment he/she is in without the interference or influences of the mind itself. This exercise will only take a few minutes a day, it's very simple, and doesn't need any sort of extravagant ritual. It is something that will be easy for beginners and aspiring Thelemites to follow. In fact, you don't have to be a member of any occult, or do this with the precesence of other fellow Thelemites. Any person can practice and apply Crowley's teachings through this simple exercise.

Quiet Awareness Exercise

Here are some steps you need to follow and keep in mind before, during, and after doing such exercise so that you can maximize this training and make it more effective.

- You should make sure that you're in a comfortable position because you'll need to maintain that for a period of time. You don't need to do any kind of yoga position or something like that, sitting still in a chair, floor, or wherever you'll feel comfortable in will do.

- You may want to also pick a location or environment that's free from any sort of distraction like loud music, television, other people etc. Once you've already gotten used to this kind of technique, you may in the future want to try doing it even if there's some distractions around but for starters, choose a relatively quiet place so that you can focus on this.

- You may also want to consider using 'props' to aid you in this exercise although it's not really necessary but if you want sort of set the mood, you can do so by lighting up some candles (not artificial light), closing the lights (if you prefer a dimmer vibe), or burning some incense to set the ambience.

- Once you're now positioned, keep in mind that you have to sit still as much as you can and try not to really move so that you can focus on your breath. Don't be too stiff either rather strive to just relax as you do this. It depends on you if you want your eyes close or open as long as you don't let it get distracted into something or wander around some object.

- When doing breathings, it's up to you if you want to count your breath. Some people do that as well just to encourage having sort of a rhythm. You can do a simple one, two, three, four breathing up to cycles of ten, or you can also do a compound count breathing (1 – 2 – 3 – 4, and out to 2 – 2 – 3 – 4). Other people prefer to not create a breathing rhythm and just let their breath settle by itself. Such things are entirely up to you as long as you're comfortable with what you're doing.

- Once you've relaxed and you're already somewhat aware of your breathing, you should in a few minutes already be in a state of deep relaxation. Sometimes this can be easily achieved after enough practice, perhaps about a week or two.

- You don't need to do this exercise for a long period of time. Ideally, 15 to 30 minutes every day will do. You don't need to overstrain or let it last for more than an hour. It might be helpful if you can also set up an alarm so that you'd be aware that you're exercise time is up, and so that you won't be distracted in watching the clock.

- Once you've already set up the physical necessities, you can now proceed on the practice proper. Practicing being aware is not about focusing on anything but it's more of just paying attention to what's happening around you. If you happened to hear someone say something, or a dog barking in the distance, you shouldn't attempt to label such sensations, just be aware that you're experiencing them.

- The same goes if you feel other things like your body tensing up or the wind against your face, or an itch. You should just accept such sensations for what they are, and not focus on it.

- Your mind at some point may began to wander, and when it does, just be aware of it and try not to get frustrated because you can't maintain such level of awareness. Just acknowledge that your mind wandered off, and slowly bring it back to awareness. Your thoughts should also just be accepted and not something to be argued with. If in case you feel your mind getting bored, try not to give in to such feeling but instead be aware that your mind is feeling some form of boredom. Try not to *be* bored but rather just experience such boredom.

- Keep doing this every day and just really try to not react to anything that your mind sets into, just be aware of it, and experience such sensations. This method is all about practicing being in existence. There's no result or outcome to look forward to, just sit still, be aware of whatever's happening inside out, and just focus on the existing moment.

Doing such exercise will eventually lead you in experiencing being aware of the conscious individual that you are. If you successfully do this, you'll soon notice how aware your mind is, and how much it tends to focus on its own creations rather than the reality of existence. Don't even think about trying to improve such practice; keep in mind, you're goal is to just be aware and not achieve anything more than that. If you feel like your mind is always wandering off, don't entertain the idea of not letting it wander off, and instead just accept whatever impressions it produce. In time, your ability to maintain such awareness will naturally improve but the purpose of Quiet Awareness Exercise is to not get better at it. Just simply do it.

The reason is that thoughts of progress are an intrusion of the mind itself. You can never practice maintaining such awareness if your mind is not inclined to retreat from awareness in the first place. That's the point of this exercise.

Simply being aware will enable you to separate yourself off of the vagaries of your mind, and on the other hand, it's also the quintessential expression of your True Will because you're not doing anything, you're just simply being the individual that you are. Just let you be, so to speak.

Most people who maintain this simple exercise find themselves wanting to continue it permanently which is good especially if you're serious about learning the core principle of Thelemic Magick. Some people want to do 'advance practices' and doesn't want to deal with the boring, ordinary and simple basics. However, you have to understand that basic means it is fundamental. Basic practices such as Quiet Awareness may indeed be boring but it's very important because it's the foundation of discovering one's True Will.

Keep in mind that mastery of the basic skills is what constitutes a master. Advance practices or techniques are made up of basic skills that one has already become a master on which is why it comes across as easy. Some people already want to learn the advance techniques without becoming a master of the basics. They may feel that they are 'advanced' but in reality, they're really not and will never be if they hadn't mastered the basic principles such as this simple awareness practice.

Chapter Four: Active Awareness

The Quiet Awareness practice aims to develop the skill or ability of awareness; of transferring the attention away from one's mind, and being aware about one's external environment. Through this basic practice, you the aspiring Thelemite will have taught yourself on how to identify what's real from the imaginary but this exercise only taught you on how to do this while you're sitting, undisturbed, and in a relax state. The next exercise is to extend such awareness into your everyday life with all the 'distractions' of the outside world. In Buddhism, they call this practice as 'mindfulness' or just being in the moment. In this chapter, we'll call it Active Awareness. It's kinda like the next level.

What is Active Awareness

The goal for this exercise is to take any moment in your life to bring the quiet awareness you have developed, and be able to bear or maintain it from moment to moment. You can do this exercise any time of the day for either a short period or a long period of time depending on you. Though we advise that you do it gradually, there's no point in hurrying.

Activities that are part of your daily routine are ideal for this exercise. For example, whenever you're taking a bath in the morning, instead of just doing it or showering to get cleaned while you're thinking about other things like how your day will go or the work you'll have to do later on, why not shower or take a bath in order to just really shower. Be aware of the sensations that you'll experience while you're doing this activity like how the water will run through you or the warmth of the water on your skin. Look at the soap as it flows through in your hands and body, and feel the sensation as you rinse yourself. Deliberately shower is what we're saying here. Take a bath for the sake of taking a bath not because you need to clean yourself or because it's a chore you have to get through. Try to slow it down, whatever activity or routine you're doing every day. Take the time to spend this moment so that you can experience what's actually happening while you're doing it. This is what 'being' instead of just 'doing' is all about. As what some people say "we are human beings, not human doings" yet the latter is what we always do.

Another common and daily routine in which you can apply active awareness or mindfulness is whenever you're eating. Lots of people just eat food because they want to relieve their hunger while their minds are not aware of the experience that they're actually eating, some are doing it so fast that they don't even know how the food taste. What you can do is to take the time to experience eating while observing or becoming aware of the sensations you'll experience during this activity. The point here is to not become too focused or conscious of your actions rather just experience your being at the moment.

Whenever you're taking a walk or you're going to work, instead of rushing through and just let everything pass you by, why not walk with mindfulness? I'm not saying slow down your walking to the point that you're going to be late for work, you can actually be mindful even if you're in a hurry. Allot time for everything, if you only have 10 to 15 minutes in the shower, or to eat, or to get to work then have a schedule, you can be mindful even if you only have a few minutes. The key however is to be aware while you're doing all of it. You can walk fast but you can still notice the people passing you by, the clouds above, the trees around, and the details in the environment around you. You can look at how the sun shines in your face, and feel how the wind touches your skin. Just like what you did in the quiet awareness exercise, the key here is to just be aware of it. Just feel it. Don't judge, don't think, just observe and acknowledge, and perhaps appreciate. If you can do this every day, you'll be surprised as to the wealth of details you'll notice even in the smallest of moments. Such details may not be something you've known before even if you're walking that same street for probably a thousand times already, and that's because you're not aware, you're not noticing such things.

You see, there's a depth of richness in even the simplest situation at any given moment. It's just waiting for us to notice it but because we don't deliberately pay attention, we miss out on all these beautiful details.

Keep in mind though that even if such exercise may generate a sense of wonder to you, the purpose of it is to just maintain your state of awareness. Proper mindfulness will enable you to observe the onset of any sensation at any given moment. As you may now know, the opportunities to become aware are limitless, and the more you practice it, the closer you get in being aligned with your True Will.

Chapter Five: Awareness of Thought

The purpose of the two practices (Quiet Awareness and Active Awareness) is to develop or unlock your skill of awareness, of perceiving what's happening in the external environment that's free from the influence of one's mind. As far as the 'self' is concerned, the scope of external isn't just comprised of the outside environment; your body and mind are also considered as external to the self. The third technique that's essential in knowing your Will. The focus this time is to turn awareness towards your mind particularly towards your thoughts. This is what we're going to teach you in this chapter.

The Awareness of Thought Technique

In the practice of mindfulness or active awareness, aspiring Thelemites like yourself learned how to notice the details and observe it right in the moment of that particular activity. Like for example whenever you're brushing your teeth, instead of just going straight to doing that, you'll be more attentive and observant this time.

For this third technique, what we're going to do is to make you be mindful of your own mind. You'll learn how to observe your mind and your thoughts, and still be free from the distortions being created by it.

We will use our previous example which was your rowboat was hit by an empty boat. As you can remember, the scenario was that you felt angry when another rowboat hit yours. Using this awareness of thought technique, you'll develop the ability to pay attention to such activity of your mind while it's happening.

So instead of 'feeling angry' or having that nudge, and immediately giving in to such emotion, what you need to do is to catch yourself feeling that particular emotion, and impartially observing this rising feeling created by your mind. Just like what you did in quiet and active awareness techniques, your job is to just observe and become aware of such feeling being created at the moment. Let's go to other more concrete examples.

Another great example is whenever your boss yells at you. You may feel angry, frustrated, incompetent or all of it. You'll then develop such feelings of resentment towards this particular boss of yours, and maybe you'll think thoughts like "How dare he talk to me like that?" or "I hate his guts, I never wanted to do this work anyway." Or perhaps something like "I'm a failure," "I'm not good enough." Such thoughts will eventually lead to other wild thoughts about your boss or about yourself/ performance.

If you want to apply the awareness of thought technique in scenarios or events similar to this, what you should do instead of identifying yourself with such emotions, or instead of believing such thoughts, you should simply be aware of them. Observe the thoughts (whether positive or negative) as they arise at the moment.

We are all guilty of easily projecting to the world whatever our mind tells us especially when our emotions run high. It's so easy to see 'bad' in people, and even in objects (just like the empty rowboat). This technique is best applied during such rising of emotions and thoughts. The awareness of thought technique aims for the self to identify and detect when the mind is doing precisely that.

If you have developed the ability to maintain awareness using the first two techniques we taught you, this third technique is going to become easier in time. The two practices aforementioned are necessary if you want to achieve such awareness of thoughts. Keep in mind though that the goal is still the same, you're not supposed to argue with your thoughts or judge such activities or even control them. Your job is to just observe, pay attention, and become aware of it as if you don't care at all, as if you're just watching a television show (you don't particularly care about).

If you happen to become aware of your thoughts, and catch yourself getting angry for example, and then you get angry because you caught yourself feeling as such, then you're missing the point. Any tendency to evaluate such mental activities or judge them is precisely what you need to be aware of for you to identify how your mind works. And once you do, you're going to eventually become aware of the contents of your mind that you may never know before.

Doing this exercise might reveal the contents of your mind including the things you don't like. For example, for a long time, you see yourself as someone who's strong or fearless but applying this practice may reveal to you that on certain occasions, you're not as fearless or strong as you think. You'll notice that at times, even if you're feeling confident, you'll still feel nervous or something. Again, you should just accept such observations. Don't try to reject it nor doubt yourself immediately because it's in conflict with your self – image. This is precisely how your mind represents such reactions. This is the reason why you shouldn't prefer one over the other; don't reject the feeling, and don't give in to it either. Don't make any preferences, just observe and be aware of such feelings because after all, it's not you, it's your mind's own preferences.

Needless to say, this practice should be approach as if you're looking the mind of another person; how it works, and how it comes up with reactions to any events occurring. You're just watching it as it go, and frankly you're just aware of what's happening as it happens. You're mindful but neutral, not favoring one over the other.

As you become better at this technique of observing how your mind works, you'll naturally tend to identify with your 'self' more and less with your mind. Identifying with your mind or blindly giving in to whatever it comes up with is usually an oversight and mostly as error. If you can become increasingly aware of how your mind works, and how you come up with thoughts and feelings, you'll be able to distinct yourself from your own mind, and more towards to your actual 'self' or True Will. Your mind will then lose its ability or power to 'fool' you.

Chapter Six: Observing the Will

The previous practices shouldn't be rushed. Keep in mind that to get better at something, anything then you need to just keep doing it over a period of time. It has to be something that's of second nature to you. The mind or the brain is perhaps the most complex organ in the body, and uncovering its hidden features or abilities will surely take time and repeated experience through practice. It's not something that a beginner will just do for a few months or even years! Training your mind takes a lifetime.

Only through continued application under various settings can somewhat make your mind better at being mindful. Time will come that your 'self' will stop paying attention to the mind, and will be more observant of your True Will. Then and only then, can you truly say that you're not attending to your mind anymore but rather to your Will.

The Art of Observing the Will

Observing one's will is an active process. This fourth technique will naturally come to you if you have already mastered or continuously applying in your daily life, the last three techniques we taught you (Quiet Awareness, Active Awareness, and Awareness of Thoughts).

As what we've mentioned at the start of this book, the core principle of Thelemic practice is 'doing one's will,' and for an aspiring Thelemite to do that, he/she must learn to become proficient in observing his mind so that he/she is paying less attention to its distortive nature. Once an aspirant learns this art, he/she can progressively be more attentive to his/her True Will. This is what we mean and perhaps what Aleister Crowley mean when it comes to discovering your Will. It's not something you find or figure out, it's something that's already naturally within you, and the only way to know your will is to clear off your own mind through mindfulness thus revealing your 'self' or True Will.

What will happen is that over time, you'll be able to observe the interactions between your external environment (including your mind) and your 'self.' You'll eventually notice the patterns of such interactions in an impartial yet clear way. If you go look out and search for these patterns, or if you actively search your Will, it wouldn't make sense because the mere act of seeking such Will is creating a conscious formulation of it because of your mental tendencies. In short, you'll never get to know your "actual will" because your mind is just creating one for you since you are seeking it in the first place. Your mind will just fool you that whatever it comes up with are your "true will." But in reality, it's not; it's just something that your mind made up.

This is why the previous exercises including this one is crucial as it will help you train your 'self' to not be fooled by your own mind.

What you can do to then to observe your will is to just develop the ability to perceive clearly. You'll need to wait for such patterns to naturally come clearly to you.

Having said all of this, and before we go to the more physical and philosophical aspects of Thelemic magick, you by now as an aspiring Thelemite should understand that it's unwise for you to start searching for your will through doing "advance practices" or perhaps various rituals without first spending time in learning and practicing the basics – which is the art of observing, of paying attention to the 'self,' of recognizing patterns, of perceiving clearly the interactions of oneself to its environment free from the distortion of one's mind, and of becoming mindful or fully aware of whatever you're doing at the moment.

All of the things mentioned are the basic groundwork that you need to continuously practice over time. Such practices is essential and necessary to knowing your Will, and understanding the core principle of Thelemic Magick before you even start doing rituals, and learning about other "spiritual aspects" of this occult. It's not to say that there's no point in doing other things, but you should make sure that you only do what you're inclined to do rather than what you think you need to do in the interest of just having "progress."

Chapter Seven: The Elementary Plane and Elemental Tools

In this chapter, we will be discussing about some of the basics you will encounter once you study the art of Thelemic Magick. Perhaps your leaders or teachers will elaborate more on this during your gatherings, or will apply it once they started teaching you about the ritual proper. One of the basic things about Thelemic magick is the understanding of the elementary plane, and the elemental tools that you can use to invoke such power. You'll get to also read about the names involve and their meanings.

Keep in mind though that the information provided from this chapter forward will only give you an overview of what you may need to learn about this practice, and since this book is aimed for beginners, we won't be able to touch and explain in detail everything there is to know because Aleister Crowley himself had to write volumes of books about Thelemic magick. Therefore, we highly encourage you to do further readings on such topics so that you can have an idea about the things we will discuss in the next few chapters.

Elementary Plane

We'll start with a couple of names that you'll encounter, and give you their meaning or significance in the Thelemic practice:

The first one is YHVH or Yaweh/ Jehovah. It is also known as Tetragrammaton. Yaweh is a holy name especially for Jews. It is the substitute name for the Lord Almighty. The next one is YHSHVH or Jesus, Joshua, or ISA. It is also known as Pentagrammation. These are some of the names you'll encounter when you study the Thelemic magick proper.

Elemental Weapons

Aside from the elementary plane, you'll also learn the tools that had been traditionally used in this practice and other magickal rituals. Such tools are known as Elemental Weapons.

These tools include the Wand, Cup, Dagger, Lamp, Disk etc. These tools also inspire other tools use in rituals like the "breaking of the bread" part in the Catholic Church during the Holy Mass.

The Brand/Wand imply the incense and the brassier. The cup inspires the wine, fount, and the lamp that provides a circle of light and also burns the oil of wisdom. The dagger implies the cutting of the sacrifice, and it also protects from that that's without the circle of light. The Disk implies the bread that the priest breaks, the plate and also the salt as well as a symbol of the Universe (eternity).

Such elemental weapons are also use in exorcism, invocation and evocation of the spirit which are all part of a Magickian's work (in the Catholic Church the magickian is the priest). Formulating and performing such rituals that enthrones the Spirit upon the so – called Throne of Elements is the task of the magickian. Success of such task can be symbolized by the Pentagram, which is why you may see priests or occult leaders wore such symbols because it is a sign that they are equipped and adept in the elementary plane.

Elemental Tools

These are some of the elemental tools or associated symbols use in the ordeal that you may encounter:

- Fire
- Father
- Phallus
- Salamander
- Sparks
- Wand
- Createth

- Water
- Mother
- Kties
- Undine
- Gems
- Cup
- Preserveth

- Spirit
- Angel
- Union
- Magickian
- Son
- Mind
- Sylph
- Gold
- Dagger
- Destroyeth
- Disk
- Redeemeth

- Nothing
- Lamp
- Writeth
- Air
- Earth
- Daughter
- Body
- Gnomes
- Silver

The associated symbols mentioned should be understood well enough to those who will use it. Otherwise, the Magickian can be 'destroyed' if he/she is not adept in using such elemental tools because these tools have sufficient power. Only an adept Magickian should take up the art of evocation using such elemental weapons.

The elemental weapons such as the wand, lamp, cup, disk, and dagger are tools that correspond to elementary archetypes. The Magickian who wants to learn the working of elementary plane must possess such weapons. If you join an occult that has an "Initiating Magickal Order," they might provide you with elemental weapons, and you can get a good advantage of having a balanced set to begin with. If not, you can improvise. Just make sure that the elemental weapons are properly balance, and should work as one. Otherwise, imbalanced weapons will produce faulty results.

The Wand of Fire

The Wand of Fire is used to break down food and to also cook. This is used so that humans can better absorb the food's nutrients. This tool best applies whenever meats are being cooked or grilled or fried. The fire drives away the spirit of the pig, beef, chicken etc. so that the 'life' may be absorb by us humans who will eat it.

The wand is usually represented by a straight branch that's cut from a sacred tree. The wand is usually cut and prepared through careful sanding and peeling before being consecrated.

Sometimes, the wand can also be empowered by using certain set of runes. After the rune symbols are carved in the wand, it is usually oiled using sacred oil, and wrapped up in a piece of clothing such as a red silk. After this is all done, it can now be kept in the altar or some magickal chest. The runes written on the wand vary according to traditions.

The want is used to activate, and also for the impregnation with the force and spirit in order to evolve that upon which it acts. The wand will be able to give evolution and creation upon which it acts; it can also be used to activate and empower the magickal signs.

In the early times, the wand is used as a hollow tube where fire was carried in the form of coals. The element of fire celebrates as the gifts of gods to mankind. The wand is also used as a channel stream of spiritual will, and a blasting rod.

You may learn that there are various specialized wands that were produce during the Golden Dawn, or from the other cultures. You may also encounter "special wands" that signify the 7 planets, 12 signs, the 2 lands of ancient Egypt etc.

The Cup of Water

Liquid is what the cup represents. It is use to symbolize water that we humans need in order to live. It also represents the water drawn from the Goddess of spring, as well as the water that we used while we're all inside our mother's womb that soon broke out when we were born.

Many people use a silver chalice cup especially when performing rituals like in a Gnostic Mass. In the early times, gold and silver are used because it can be reused and recycled many times. What magickians usually suggest is to always use objects that personally 'call out to you' regardless if they are reused or completely new, if you can polish them or varnish it with a new coat of silver then better. In any case, the key is to finding something that could make it personal, unique or meaningful to you.

If you happen to have a plate chalice, make sure to electroplate it with an extra silver or gold as some of the metals may be toxic. As to the design of the cup, some people choose Egyptian Lotus. The Egyptian Lotus is a style of the Golden Dawn; the lotus has blue petals. You can also use glass and ceramic designs to match such motif.

As mentioned earlier, the wand symbolizes the Will of man, so does the cup. The Cup of Water symbolizes the receptive quality of the Love of Woman. Some highest spells employ the biological counterparts of the Wand and the Cup. The Wand is the symbol of Will, and the Cup symbolizes Love. The Cup should be covered until the other elemental weapons are prepared. It should be covered, cleaned, and kept from filth. If your cup is always left uncovered then it can be receptive and exposed to unwanted things.

In special events, the liquid sacrament contained by the cup may be of other forms other than water. Sometimes it is replaced with wine which is believed as a solar liquid sacrament that contains spirits. During the times of the ancient Greece, the cup is filled with Elixir Vitae. This is a solvent that contains certain herbs that had intoxicating properties. However, should acidic wines or herbs be used, you should be careful because it might get mixed in with a non – reactive metal that's within the cup. If you invoke the cup or prepared it in an inappropriate way, you might poison yourself. Just like there are special wands, there's also special cups so better be careful.

Lamp of Spirit

Without Spirit, we wouldn't be able to see and eat the meal that signifies the body of a god or goddess. Back in the day, at the funeral of Osiris, such meal was eaten by his loved ones and relatives. The version of this practice can also be seen in the Christian sacrament or during the Holy Eucharist. All the elements gather around the lamp which represents the light, and it is in their throne where the Spirit is exalted. The lamp signifies the Spirit which humans need as a guide in discovering the will. As you may know, light is what we need in times of darkness. We become enlightened by the Holy Guardian Angel for without the light, no work can be done.

After the rituals and consecration, the lamp must be ideally wrapped up and placed into an altar. If you happen to have a silver candlestick, then make sure to wrap it in black silk after being anointed in white silk. Spirit is passive and also active.

You can also use a camp lantern or a candle placed within a glass as your "magick lamp" so that the wind doesn't blow off the light during ritual performances. Be careful if you're going to use oil because if you knocked it off, fire will spread out since there are also cloths around during your rites. Consider having a fire extinguisher around just in case. If you wanted to use oil lamps, make sure to adjust the wick so that it will just give an appropriate amount of light. Avoid using scented lamp oils unless you need the fragrance for some magickal purposes.

Each component of the lamp has an equivalent archetypal meaning; traditionally, olive oil is what people use but the downside is that it produces lots of smoke. If you still wish to use such type of oil, make sure to buy the U.S.P. Olive Oil.

Just like cups and wands, there are also special spirit lights and lamps that come with varying colors which can help in harmonizing certain vibrations. Candle sticks and spirits as well as the certain oils, colors, and shapes of candles are believed to also call to upon particular forces. Ancient Egyptians symbolize the stars as the "lamps of the sky" back then.

Dagger of Air

The dagger of air represents the power to divide, and also to banish. The mind divides things into categories, and in the same way, the mind partake into the symbolism of this archetype.

Magickians usually engrave words in their daggers that represent the universe. Some magickians use either light or dark color handles in their knives which also symbolizes the air.

The Wand symbolizes the Father; the Cup represents the Mother, the Lamp symbolizes the Spirit or the light in between the Wand and Cup; the dagger then represents the Son which is the symbol of their conjunction. The Wand is active and reactive, but the dagger is active and divisive because it cuts things.

Acquiring or manufacturing your own unique dagger could be difficult as there are lots of designs you can choose from, making it hard to determine what best fits you, so to speak. Whenever you're going to bring or use a knife to do your rituals, make sure that you're not violating any law. Check first the law regarding bringing of weapons. If you're just going to do rituals in your own house then you won't have any problem as long as you keep it safe from other people.

Some magickians manufacture their own knives because they want a certain shape or a certain kind of steel. Other magickians just buy a ready - made dagger, and engrave runic symbols upon it.

After consecrating the dagger through symbols such as runes, you need to wrap it with yellow silk and place it in your magick chest or in an altar. You can also acquire special daggers in the form of an ax, swords, or an engraver; it still

functions in the same way which is that it cuts and divides.

Disk of Earth

The Disk represents the power to embody a form,

power to crystallize, and it is also the solid state of matter.

Sometimes it can be represented by a coin of the realm, or a

plate of bread/ cakes. Cups are creative and passive, disks or

coins on the other hand are also passive, or perhaps

receptive but quite divisive. Coins are usually used to divide

in proportions and also be compared to something that is of

value. The dividing according to something's worth is the

coin's inherent value, and such value is the work done to

deserve a coin. As the old saying goes, "The true cost of

something, is the amount of life you expend in getting it."

Coins or disks are just like cups, the difference

however is that the cup holds the actual worthy thing while

coins contains the equivalent value of the task done.

When designing this elemental tool, you can use a stamp or engrave what you desire. You can also prepare a design of wax or create a replica of some ancient coin found in museums, and have it cast, plated or struck upon your coin. Traditionally, people use silver, copper, and gold so it's up to you what you prefer or what best resonates with you. Aside from this you can also use photographic technique to use in your design. It's best that the pattern or design you use is a symbol for the Universe.

Chapter Eight: The Holy Guardian Angel

Now that you know the basic core principle behind this practice, and you have learned how you can discover your True Will by becoming more mindful, of becoming more aware, we're now going to discuss one of the most important basic aspects of Thelema Magick which is the knowledge and conversation of the Holy Guardian Angel.

Explaining this subject matter is one of the most difficult things to do. I actually feel that sometimes this was a cosmic joke for me and others like me who are attempting to explain such concept because it's quite impossible to fully explain this kind of topic, so please do me a favor and just bear with me if ever I use inevitably inadequate language to explain such concept.

The HGA

The "Holy Guardian Angel" is a term that Aleister Crowley used. According to him, the holy guardian angel pertains to the experience, a higher being, an aspect of 'self,' or perhaps a sort of an external entity. In other religions, traditions, and mystic practices, it's something related to the higher self, the Universe, the higher genius, conscience, 'gut feel' or "god".

Crowley talked about the concept of holy guardian angel throughout his life, and he relates it depending on who his audience is at the moment; he also talked about it in different phases of his life. Sometimes he described it as if it was something similar to the higher self which is according to him an aspect of our own conscious and subconscious existence, while other times he refer to the holy guardian angel as some sort of external entity through the form of an external voice dictating him what to write in his The Book of the Law.

Let's delve a bit deeper and talk about how an aspirant like yourself can experience the HGA as it tends to manifest in your life.

One of the most common misconceptions about how the HGA experience occurs in people is that there's no conscious connection or concrete knowledge of the holy guardian angel, and if ever there is, it is something that anyone can just suddenly 'experience.' For instance, whenever you say like, "oh I've heard the voice of God telling me what to do," some people will interpret it as if, God just suddenly communicated with you. Now some people may have experience such a phenomenon but for most people, it's gradual.

There is a gradual intimacy of understanding and communicating which usually begins at the start of your journey of communicating with God or whoever your 'higher being' is. It's usually a courtship. It's a gradually intensifying and increasing intimacy. It's a gradual improving of your ability to perceive the language of the HGA in your life until such a point where your 'self' has already formed a conscious link and where you can already communicate with it consciously and at will.

Process of Conversing with Your HGA

So what's this process like? How can one start this courtship or intimacy with the HGA? It's a process where one can differentiate or identify the one voice of the angel from all the other voices that our minds probably made up, or the voices that speak to us in different ways in our lives. It's like what we've talked about in discovering your True Will. You have to be able to cleanse your mind so that True Will can be revealed. Identify what is it that your mind told you is your "Will" and what is your actual Will through awareness, mindfulness or observation.

When it comes to communicating with the HGA, it's kind of similar to a radio frequency. Whenever you're trying to find the right radio station, what you'll usually hear at first as you turn the dial is that static sound. Sometimes you get pass it, and you'll just hear a snippet of sound from that particular station or DJ you like, and then you get lost and will try to go through all the buzzing static sounds again, until you fine tune and clearly hear the radio station you prefer. The overall process of communicating and experiencing the holy guardian angel is quite akin to this. You're searching for that ability to tune in to that station and keep it there.

It's actually less about finding where the holy guardian angel is, or looking where your True Will is, it's more of finding yourself and getting yourself in the right place to perceive the HGA, or your True Will that's just waiting for you to discover them.

Many people think that the process of knowing and experiencing or conversing with your HGA depends on the proper invocation of the angel or it's highly dependent on following specific instructions or methods, but that's not the case. Everything you have been, everything you are, and everything you will become is going to be utilized in your path. All of your past, present and future experiences will be your tools that you need in order to invoke your own holy guardian angel. As you move along your journey, you'll eventually learn how to improve through certain methods that your teachers will present to you, and be able to naturally tune your ability to invoke the holy guardian angel.

There are many tools and methods that you'll learn depending on what organization you'll join, or who your leaders/ teachers will be. Some may fit you but some may perhaps be alien to you, regardless, you should still keep an open mind and experiment or learn from it anyway because it'll strengthen those parts of you that might not be as much of a natural inclination. Navigating from such dry spells or mystical methods that doesn't resonate well with you is all part of the work but keep in mind that it will still help you in strengthening yourself which will enable you to complete your training.

Most experienced Thelemites will suggest that the best way to practice is to constantly invoke often and inflame yourself in prayer. Such method can make the core of yourself respond well, and will inevitably lead you in the right path.

Development of Relationship with HGA

The process is simple, like anything else in life; you just really have to forge ahead with the grey task, keep invoking often and immersing yourself in prayer, keep pushing towards the path of knowledge and conversation to your HGA and devoting yourself. Such acts will inevitably lead you to naturally get the layers of instruction, or an impulse to pursue something, and perhaps have your own unique ritual format. After putting in the effort, you may find later on that you'll learn something that'll supersede the instructions that was previously given to you before because this is the nature of such work.

As you refine the tools of reception or fine tuning that one voice, it'll be a naturally process to set aside or perhaps let go of some of the things you've learn (I guess some people may call it as the process of unlearning). However, just don't let your self – doubt interfere with certainty that if you persist, you'll refine your own tools and be able to clearly hear the voice of your holy guardian angel at will.

Chapter Nine: Daily Magickal Regimen

This chapter is going to cover the basics of daily magickal ritual or magickal regimen. Some of you may have already started doing your own magickal regimens or may have already experimented with it, but I think it is still necessary for you to learn an overview of the kind of magickal practices available to you as a beginner, and it's also essential for you to know the reason why you should adapt a certain practice.

You'll find that there are lots of resources out there that will help you when it comes to knowing the basic magickal rituals, the fundamental ritual performances, the various magickal exercises you can do etc. but there's usually a gap, and the gap is simply knowing why a practitioner need to choose a certain magickal regimen.

Lots of aspiring Thelemites usually end up having the overall goal of "being the best and powerful magickian" while this is of course a good goal for every aspirant, this is still something vague and immeasurable, so to speak. That kind of goal setting is actually not the best way to start any endeavor simply because it's not specific enough and it's too broad. Like any other things in life that you want to achieve or accomplish anything, proper goal setting is important. Breaking down your goal into something achievable and measurable is a great way for you to improve your magick skills. This chapter will enlighten you further by knowing what your ritual goals are, what specific skills that you're trying to build, and what specific practices are available to you that you can work with and maximize in order to get better at this craft.

The things that we're going to talk about or the tips that we'll suggest that you try is on the assumption that you're a beginner, and you haven't joined a particular organization yet that has specific assigned magick tasks or practices. If ever you are, we highly advised that you consult your teacher first as to the kind of additional magickal regimen or any changes that you may want to adapt after reading this chapter, just so it wouldn't have any conflict or something. If you're not working in any system or if your organization is open to you adapting other practices like what we will discuss here, then read on.

Basic Training Goals for Beginners

For a beginning magickian like yourself, you need to have sort of what we call "magickal hygiene," this is like the Thelema magick equivalent of brushing your teeth. You need to have a set of practices that will cleanse your energy system; it could either pertain to your aura, psychology, or however you want to define your energy system.

One of your major goals is to know how to build your ability to call forth the magickal force, to tolerate such magickal force, and also the ability to direct the magickal force to the aims that you might have established. If you put this in the context of studying yoga, this magickal hygiene is similar to knowing the basics; the kind of posture you need to have, or the position you need to be in because such things will help you focus better and direct that attention to whatever you set your mind into.

You need to begin internalizing magickal symbol systems into your daily magickal work routine. You need to internalize, not just read or memorize, but to really understand the basic concepts of magick like the Tree of Life which is what you can model your psyche or your 'self' into. You need to internalize the various correspondences that are related to your magickal work. You need to find a way to build these symbols and make it part of your daily life routine.

In short, you need to live and breathe with it, just like how great athletes do. For instance, if you want to be a great or skilled basketball player in the NBA, you just don't practice during training, or before a big game. Usually, even if it's an off – season, basketball superstars still practice shooting both in the court, and in their minds/ lives. They eat with it, sleep with it, and breathe with their skill. It's not work to them, it's not even a ritual or something that they need to give time to; basketball is their life, basketball is them. The mindset and skills that they've built enables them to still 'play' even if they aren't playing or aren't holding a ball. As an aspiring magickian, this is your ultimate goal, to make the magickal system one with you. You have to find a way to incorporate magick into your daily life. If you know how to do that, conversing with your Holy Guardian Angel, and acting based on your True Will is something that will come easy to you, or perhaps already second – nature to you.

Your basic magickal training should start to forge that conscious link that we've talked about in the previous chapters, and immerse yourself in 'prayer' however you want to define it; the key is immersing yourself into these trainings. These are the reasons why you need to be completely devoted to such practices because it'll help you build your 'magickal muscles,' and will inevitably lead you in the right direction.

Different Phases of Magickal Ritual Training

This section will guide you on how to achieve such magickal goals, and how you can set up the practices to achieve them. You'll also get to learn the different phases of this practice training so that you can understand it better.

The basic training that'll be described in this book consists mainly of four phases. Some of the training phases will need a few weeks to practice while some need a few months. The set of training that you're going to learn is still part of the basic practices since you're still a beginner, but keep in mind that there are still a lot of practices you need to learn other than what you will get to know in this section.

Phase 1

The most fundamental and essential practice that you need to learn in this phase is your ability to be free of external distractions, and learn to relax your body. I know this sound like a boring practice, and it's not something that newbies or aspirants like you will be excited about but like what we've discuss in the previous chapters, before you learn the more exciting or advance magickal techniques, you need to be able to master the basics because these are the foundations of those 'advance techniques.'

Controlling your level of relaxation and/ or arousal will definitely help you in attempting to control other less uncontrollable things later on as we discuss further. If you can't control your own impulses, your own focus then how can you achieve directing a magickal force? This is such an important fundamental and 'magickal muscle' that you need to become a master at. It's simple, it's boring, and soon you'll find that it's not easy. It may look easy because all you need to do is to relax and clear your mind, but as you take the time to do this, you might find yourself being distracted by almost anything. This is somewhat similar to the kind of the basic exercises you did in the first few chapters about observing the mind or becoming aware of your thoughts. You need to learn how to calm down and relax even if your own mind is distracting you or your emotions are rising.

So what you need to do for phase 1 is to just sit or lie down for a few minutes, and free your mind from the distractions or concerns of the external world. This is how you should start every practice session for this phase. You need to let go and just be.

As you settle in, you're going to need to start doing some breathing exercise. This won't just help you in the whole process of relaxation; it will also help you focus your mind into one thing – your breathing. You don't need to focus on breathing patterns or rhythms because it will naturally be on the beat or on point. Focus on getting the air you inhale from your nose through your diaphragm and exhale it out, and eventually you'll develop a certain breathing rhythm or pattern. This exercise will help you to improve your ability to control your energy that's present in each breath you take. So as you can see, it's not just about relaxation or proper breathing or posture, this is about your ability to be mindful and control energy.

We suggest you start doing this for a few weeks on a daily basis, it's nothing fancy but it's essential. I know it's not what a beginner like expect when it comes to studying Thelema magick but I can guarantee that this simple relaxation and breathing exercise will transform you mentally, emotionally, physically, and will help you throughout your magickal journey or career. I urge you to do this well, and do it right because this is what's going to make you a powerful magickian. It's all in the basics.

Phase 2

After a few weeks of mastering Phase 1, you can now add some things and move on to Phase 2. In Phase 2, you need to learn about the invoking and banishing forms of a lesser ritual of the Pentagram. The invoking part of the Pentragram ritual will help build your tolerance for energy, enhance your ability to call it forth and also channel the energy into things like visualizations, rituals, drawing of the pentagrams etc. because all of these things represent your mind, and will serve as the channel of that particular energy that you're calling or shaping.

Through exercises like these, you'll start to learn how to internalize the energy or the rituals, the correspondences, the holy guardian angel, and associate the elements/energies with your own experience so that you can start to form your inner language about it.

So for Phase 2, before you learn the art of invoking of the lesser ritual of the Pentragram, you'll need to make yourself relax and choose any posture that you're comfortable with, and just sit still before you begin concentrating on the ritual. You'll need to just simply focus on the triangles presented in the lesser ritual of the pentagram and use your visualization to just hold that image in your mind. It may also help if you can jot down the experience you've had while doing this exercise in your magick diary.

You need to practice this for an extended period of time, or at least for about a month or two before moving to Phase 3.

Phase 3

After doing Phases 1 and 2, you can now add some form of Middle Pillar Exercise as well as circulations exercises. These exercises will help you kick your energy system up a notch in terms of tolerating energy, calling it, and directing/ controlling the magickal force. You'll get to also learn how to internalize the divine names associated with your chakras, and you'll now have tools in order to inflame yourself. The Middle of the Pillar Ritual will enable you to visualize your crown center or the chakra located on top of your head, and also let you throw yourself out to your highest being or perhaps your holy guardian angel. It will also help you begin the practice of uniting those high ideals or high forms of energy, and build that within your daily routine through devotional practice.

You can also add some form of meditations on the Sefiroth and the 'paths' which is something that you'll learn by reading Thelema books so that you can reflect on some phrases that's linked with the 22 paths of life etc.

At this point, you can see how the correspondences and the technicalities of Thelema Magick such as symbol systems will need to come together through your internalization process while you're also practicing handling the energies and controlling your 'self.'

For Phase 3, you'll need to keep on practicing the Middle of the Pillar Ritual plus internalizing the symbol systems for about 6 months or so before moving to Phase 4.

Phase 4

In this final basic phase, we suggest that you add or meditate on the traditional Lesser Ritual of the Hexagram. This is something that's related to studying the Sefiroth and the 22 paths of life. We suggest that you do it for another couple of weeks to a few months, and extend if you need to.

General Recommendations for Getting Started

Rhythm is very important.

It is one of the languages being communicated with us from our unconscious mind. If you are able to prove to your unconscious that you're tune in to it by following a certain routine or giving a time for it, your unconscious and your spiritual system will sort of be in 'sync' so to speak, compared to just practicing at random times and having to deal with interferences throughout the day. For you to do this, we suggest that you practice at least 6 days a week and just give yourself a day off to build it in.

You don't need to spend too much time every day to perform the different phases or study the rituals we've mentioned but just give yourself time for it otherwise it'll be strenuous for you as a beginner, and you're basically setting yourself up for failure. If you can take at least an hour a day to practice the rituals and the techniques at a constant time that'll be enough to start inculcating in to your system. It will help you to essentially create a routine.

Consider Using a Magickal Diary

We suggest that you also use 'magickal diary' or an electronic type of diary so that it'll be more convenient for you to pull out whenever you need to jot down magickal notes. This can be an app in your phone or it can be done in your laptop, tablet etc. through word processing programs. Some magickians prefer a personal journal or a physical diary that they can carry with them so it's up to you what you like. However, the advantages of having an electronic diary are that you can easily and immediately search keywords and passages from across the many days or months that you've been documenting. It will also be easier for you to pull out certain ritual exercises and entries that you've done and would want to review.

Aside from that you'd be able to easily keep track of what you've accomplished so far and sort of compile them up or consolidate it. Having an electronic diary is more convenient since some things aforementioned are quite difficult to do if you keep a paper diary but of course, it's still your choice.

The important thing is to use a 'magickal' diary that will function as your notepad so that the activities, practices, and lessons you've had is well – documented.

Make sure to do your diary entry after finishing up whatever ritual or practices that you're doing on that day. Write down your notes, observations, conclusions etc. as soon as possible so that you won't forget, and while you're still not essentially distracted by your conscious state because some details might already be left out if you write it at a later time.

I'm also here to remind you that one way or another, you're going to mess up your rituals and your schedules, and there'll be days where you won't be able to accomplish what you need to do in your daily Thelema practice for various reasons. Regardless, you still need to document and keep a diary on that day that simply state the reason why you're not able to do your training today (ex: you got distracted, family emergency, you got lazy today etc.). Don't worry because you don't have to apologize for it, or beat yourself up as it can happen to anyone, anytime. The important thing is to just keep the discipline of documenting it in your 'magickal' diary because it might come in handy when you're reviewing your work, and perhaps you'll find patterns as to why you have or have not done your work.

Fear and Shame is never helpful

You don't need to beat yourself up for the things you did and didn't do. Don't be afraid to experiment different practices or rituals, and most importantly don't be scared of doing trial and error because that's the way everything works. When you do fail at something, try to document it on your diary in detail. Record what you've done, what you think went wrong, and the lessons you've had for creating such mistake.

This will help you improve and get better. Like anything else in life, it's okay to fail. In fact, failure in any endeavor is a requirement because it's only through failure that one will succeed and get better, and learn more. As long as you're doing the basic practices we've described in this book or the rituals/ training system that your organization taught you, you're unlikely to run into serious trouble.

Fortifying yourself with the basic Thelema practices will enable you to have strength and courage whenever you set yourself out and try other methods or more 'advanced' trainings.

Chapter Ten: Integrating Magickal Practices in Daily Life

In this chapter, we'll discuss about other subtle magickal or ritual techniques that goes beyond the usual basic magickal regimen. We will discuss ways on how you can stay being mindful of your magickal path and your Will. We will also give you ideas on how you can incorporate small ritual exercises into your daily experience so that no matter what you're doing or where you are, you can still integrate the magickal techniques into your life. We're also going to cover various categories including mindfulness techniques, Eucharistic principles, breath awareness techniques, sexual techniques, and the likes. This can serve as your 'magickal toolbox' that you can use in your everyday life.

Eucharist Practices

There are really no limitations on how an aspirant or a Thelemite magickian can integrate the concept of the Eucharist into one's daily life. In terms of Thelemic approach, you can read about the Gnostic Mass, and see as to how you can adapt the process of ritual and perhaps have your own 'mini mass.' You can do a mini ritual by yourself every day by consecrating the elements which is your wine and host (just like how Christians do it during the Holy Eucharist). You can walk yourself through this process, and learn how to invoke the divine force while you're combining the elements before consuming them.

Aside from this you can also add in visualization techniques, and also combine it with the benefit of performing the Eucharist rituals aforementioned.

Many of you aspiring Thelemites might have already come across the idea that you can use visualization to make your desired outcome a reality through focusing on a certain thought or the end result because doing such can increase the probability of your desired outcome materializing. Some of you may be a bit skeptical about this technique but it's good to try it and see for yourself while also binding it with the Eucharist or Gnostic Mass ritual. You need to hold in your mind the picture or vision of your desired outcome throughout the process in order to build the intensity while you're consecrating, uniting, and consuming the elements as well as invoking the divine force.

You should hold the desired outcome in mind then after consuming the Eucharist or elements that is charged with your desired outcome then you embody the end result you like to have.

The more intense and vivid your vision is of your desired outcome, the more effective it can be. You can make something vivid by injecting emotions into your visualization, or the way you will feel once you already attained that desired result, the way your life is going to be once you attained that outcome, and the way your life and that of others will take shape if you attained your end result. The more vivid the picture of your desire is, the more you will better program your neurons to be oriented in making that outcome manifest in reality.

Mindfulness Practices

The exercises of discovering your True Will as well as other mind – related techniques that we've discussed in the previous chapters are part of this mindfulness practices. You can extend such practices and concepts to any task in your daily life. Whatever you're doing during the day, can and should be recognize as a contribution of your True Will's execution. For instance, you can say that it is your Will to get in your car and go to work so that you can earn money, or help your customers; you do this because you want to have a comfortable place to live in so that you can pursue your magickal work, or further your Thelema education, expand your mind, and increase the capacity of your psyche so that it can be a vessel of your True Will. Anything you're doing is putting a service to your Will.

If ever you find that it's quite hard to explain to yourself why the things you're doing is in service of your True Will then maybe you need to rethink your routines or the activities you pursue because it may not be something that resonates, fulfills, or is in service of your True Will. This also applies even if you don't know your True Will is yet; whatever you're doing should be in one way or another be a step or path towards your desired outcome.

Another mindfulness practice and also a balancing premise of your daily life are by practicing on how you can be a 'balanced vessel' or balanced microcosm. In terms of the Pentagram, you need to be balanced of the 4 elements and the spirits. You need to practice how you can be mindful of these concepts, and find a way on how you can integrate the 4 elements and spirits in your daily routine. You have to find a way on how you can embody that balance and also be mindful of it. One way is through practicing the rituals or exercises daily and also is able to record that in your magickal diary. You can note the correspondents of the 4 elements (fire, air, water, earth) and spirit then rate yourself (ex: rate from 1 to 10) every day on how much you've embodied these elements or other Thelema concepts.

Earth: How well did I take care of my physical body today? (rate from 1 to 10)

Air: How well did I attend to my subconscious mind and/or sexuality? (rate from 1 to 10)

Water: How much emphasis did I put on in my well – functioning intellect? (rate from 1 to 10)

Fire: How did I do in order to achieve my ritual goal, or how did I do in my devotion to the holy guardian angel, to my aspirations etc.? (rate from 1 to 10)

Spirit: How receptive am I in terms of the light of the spirit manifesting through my life? Is my magickal lamp lit? (rate from 1 to 10)

If you spend each day by being mindful about the Pentagram, your thoughts, your True Will etc. you'll soon find that you can embody these exercises way better than before.

Conclusion

Following the practices that we've laid out throughout this book will surely take you a step further your journey as an aspiring Thelemite. Each exercise, each ritual, each practices, each new knowledge, and each discovery will lead you to finding your True Will. Finding your True Will will get you closer to the truth about what your true purpose is here on earth, and it will lead you and guide you on your everyday journey.

As we've mentioned before, do not limit yourself with the concepts and practices that you've learned here because the things we've discussed are just the basic of the basics, and we haven't totally scratch the surface so to speak. However, the topics you've learned here is already enough to get you started, and serves as your foundation for further knowledge about Thelema magick. You'll soon find yourself as one of them Thelemites, and with enough time, practice, and dedication, you'll definitely be a step closer to becoming a master magickian.

Photo Credits

Page 1 Photo by user Claudia Gabriela Marques via flickr.com,

https://www.flickr.com/photos/saphirai/481212735/

Page 2 Photo by user Tim Pierce via flickr.com,

https://www.flickr.com/photos/qwrrty/14552322328/

Page 11 Photo by user Hartwig HKD via flickr.com,

https://www.flickr.com/photos/h-k-d/2694276306/

Page 23 Photo by user Odysseus - Studio via flickr.com,

https://www.flickr.com/photos/mjl555/1478773099/

Page 32 Photo by user Chiaralily via flickr.com,

https://www.flickr.com/photos/chiaralily/40472861352/

Page 38 Photo by user Natalio via flickr.com,

https://www.flickr.com/photos/nmaicas/17351570126/

Page 45 Photo by user Kyla Clay via flickr.com,

https://www.flickr.com/photos/76881191@N07/15237303123/in/photolist

Page 51 Photo by user Hartwig HKD via flickr.com,

https://www.flickr.com/photos/h-k-d/2895860359/

Page 67 Photo by user Agathe LM via flickr.com,

https://www.flickr.com/photos/107920892@N02/16141991737/

Page 76 Photo by user Eddi van W. via flickr.com,

https://www.flickr.com/photos/spiritual_marketplace/2428641431/

Page 94 Photo by user ambroo via Pixabay.com,

https://pixabay.com/en/saint-meditation-yoga-meditating-198958/

References

"Magickk (Thelema)" – Wikipedia.org

https://en.wikipedia.org/wiki/Magickk_(Thelema)

"Introduction to Thelema" – KAOOS.org

http://www.kaaos.org/faerie/thelema.html

"The Science and Art of Magickk" – Thelema101.com

http://www.thelema101.com/magickk

"Introduction to Thelema" – Thelema101.com

http://www.thelema101.com/magickk-i

**"Understanding the Religion of Thelema

An Introduction for Beginners"** – Thoughtco.com

https://www.thoughtco.com/thelema-95700

"Fundamentals of Thelemic Practice" - ErwinHessle.com

http://www.erwinhessle.com/writings/thelprac.php

"Magickk in Theory and Practice" – Sacred – Texts.com

http://www.sacred-texts.com/oto/aba/aba.htm

"Thelemic Qabalah" - Astronargon.us

http://www.astronargon.us/Thelemic%20Qabalah%20Volume%201.pdf

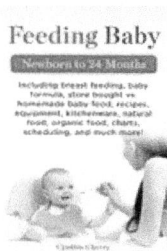

Feeding Baby
Cynthia Cherry
978-1941070000

Axolotl
Lolly Brown
978-0989658430

Dysautonomia, POTS
Syndrome
Frederick Earlstein
978-0989658485

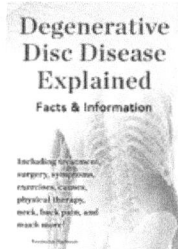

Degenerative Disc
Disease Explained
Frederick Earlstein
978-0989658485

Sinusitis, Hay Fever,
Allergic Rhinitis Explained
Frederick Earlstein
978-1941070024

Wicca
Riley Star
978-1941070130

Zombie Apocalypse
Rex Cutty
978-1941070154

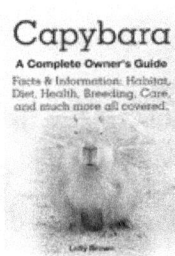

Capybara
Lolly Brown
978-1941070062

Eels As Pets
Lolly Brown
978-1941070167

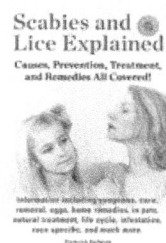

Scabies and Lice Explained
Frederick Earlstein
978-1941070017

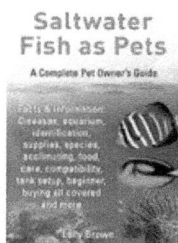

Saltwater Fish As Pets
Lolly Brown
978-0989658461

Torticollis Explained
Frederick Earlstein
978-1941070055

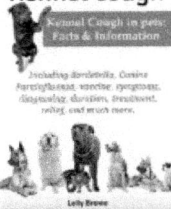

Kennel Cough
Lolly Brown
978-0989658409

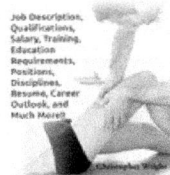

Physiotherapist, Physical
Therapist
Christopher Wright
978-0989658492

Rats, Mice, and Dormice
As Pets
Lolly Brown
978-1941070079

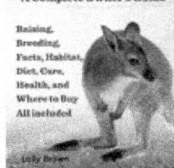

Wallaby and Wallaroo Care
Lolly Brown
978-1941070031

Bodybuilding Supplements
Explained
Jon Shelton
978-1941070239

Demonology
Riley Star
978-19401070314

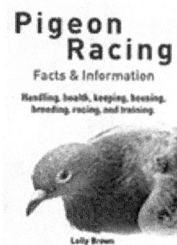

Pigeon Racing
Lolly Brown
978-1941070307

Dwarf Hamster
Lolly Brown
978-1941070390

Cryptozoology
Rex Cutty
978-1941070406

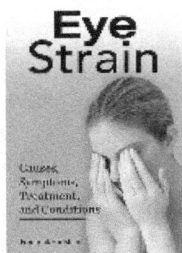

Eye Strain
Frederick Earlstein
978-1941070369

Inez The Miniature Elephant
Asher Ray
978-1941070353

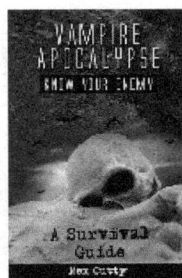

Vampire Apocalypse
Rex Cutty
978-1941070321

www.ingramcontent.com/pod-product-compliance
Lightning Source LLC
LaVergne TN
LVHW051648080426
835511LV00016B/2567